ALL ABOUT SHARKS
ENDANGERED SHARKS

by Elisa A. Bonnin

BrightPoint Press

San Diego, CA

© 2023 BrightPoint Press
an imprint of ReferencePoint Press, Inc.
Printed in the United States

For more information, contact:
BrightPoint Press
PO Box 27779
San Diego, CA 92198
www.BrightPointPress.com

ALL RIGHTS RESERVED.

No part of this work covered by the copyright hereon may be reproduced or used in any form or by any means—graphic, electronic, or mechanical, including photocopying, recording, taping, web distribution, or information storage retrieval systems—without the written permission of the publisher.

LIBRARY OF CONGRESS CATALOGING-IN-PUBLICATION DATA

Names: Bonnin, Elisa A., author.
Title: Endangered sharks / by Elisa A. Bonnin.
Description: San Diego, CA: BrightPoint Press, [2023] | Series: All about sharks | Includes bibliographical references and index. | Audience: Grades 10-12
Identifiers: LCCN 2022016076 (print) | LCCN 2022016077 (eBook) | ISBN 9781678203641 (hardcover) | ISBN 9781678203658 (pdf)
Subjects: LCSH: Sharks--Conservation--Juvenile literature. | Endangered species--Juvenile literature.
Classification: LCC QL638.9 .B67 2023 (print) | LCC QL638.9 (eBook) | DDC 597.3--dc23/eng/20220413
LC record available at https://lccn.loc.gov/2022016076
LC eBook record available at https://lccn.loc.gov/2022016077

CONTENTS

AT A GLANCE ... 4

INTRODUCTION ... 6
 DANGER!

CHAPTER ONE ... 12
 BYCATCH

CHAPTER TWO ... 24
 OVERFISHING

CHAPTER THREE ... 36
 HABITAT AND HUMANS

CHAPTER FOUR ... 48
 PROTECTING SHARKS

Glossary ... 58
Source Notes ... 59
For Further Research ... 60
Index ... 62
Image Credits ... 63
About the Author ... 64

AT A GLANCE

- Sharks that are endangered or threatened are at risk of dying out, or going extinct. More than half of all shark species are endangered or threatened.

- Sharks become endangered for many reasons. Three of these are bycatch, overfishing, and human activity.

- Fisheries often catch sharks accidentally. That's known as bycatch. Fishing tools called longlines and gillnets are especially harmful to sharks.

- To reduce bycatch, fisheries can be more careful about what they catch.

- Some people catch sharks on purpose. Humans in many parts of the world eat shark meat. People fish for sharks for fun too.

- Shark finning, or catching sharks just for their fins, is a harmful form of shark fishing. Shark finning has led to hammerhead sharks becoming critically endangered.

- Pollution can also harm sharks by making their habitats harder to live in.

- Some large sharks are harmed by commercial shipping routes when large ships strike and kill them.

- Governments around the world are making laws to ban shark finning and create shark sanctuaries to help shark populations recover.

- Sharks are important to the ocean ecosystem. Protecting sharks helps keep the ocean healthy.

INTRODUCTION

DANGER!

A great white shark follows the scent of prey. A school of fish swims up ahead, scales flashing in the sunlight. Their scent fills the water. The shark moves forward, its powerful muscles cutting through the water. It has almost reached its prey.

Suddenly, a net stops the shark from reaching the fish. The shark tries to back away, and the net gets caught on its gills. The shark tries to break free, but it's no use. It can hardly breathe. Humans try to

A great white swims near a group of fish.

untangle the shark, but it is too late. The shark dies.

ENDANGERED SHARKS

Sharks are some of the most well-known marine creatures. Many humans think sharks are unstoppable predators. But sharks can be harmed or killed. In fact, more than half of all shark species are **endangered** or threatened. That means there are far fewer of these sharks than there used to be. And their numbers keep shrinking. Many shark species are in danger of going extinct, or dying out.

A fisher catches a blacktip shark in Oman, a country in the Middle East.

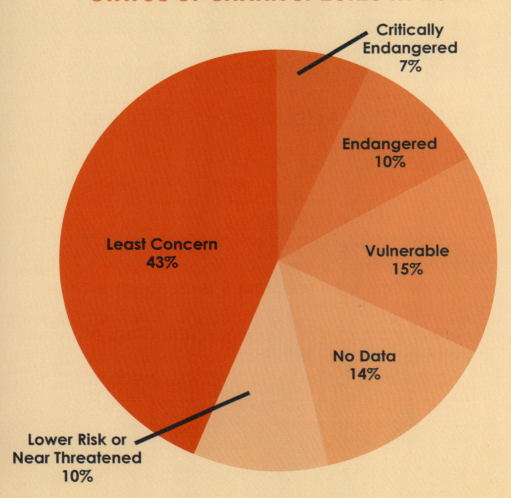

This pie chart shows the conservation status of shark species in 2021. The numbers are rounded to the nearest percent, which means they won't total exactly 100 percent.

Shark numbers are declining for several reasons. Fishing is a big one. Fisheries that sell fish often catch sharks, either accidentally or on purpose. Fishing for fun, where fishers compete to catch the biggest fish, also harms sharks. And like many marine animals, sharks are hurt by pollution or damage to their habitats. Sharks are an important part of the ocean **ecosystem**. That means people must help them stay safe and healthy. That keeps the ocean safe and healthy, too.

1

BYCATCH

The fish at the supermarket or on food menus normally comes from **commercial** fisheries. These are big companies that sell what they catch. They try to catch as many fish as possible at one time. This means they often scoop up creatures they can't sell.

The stuff that fishers accidentally catch is called **bycatch.** Sharks often end up as bycatch because they're large. They struggle to get away from nets. They're also

Fishers accidentally caught this shark along with other sea creatures.

A blacktip shark will be thrown back into the ocean after being caught.

predators, which means they tend to be near the fish that fishers want to catch.

Big fisheries report tens of millions of sharks as bycatch every year. But other fisheries are smaller. They make up 95 percent of all the fishing groups in the world. These small-scale fisheries catch 35 percent of the world's catch of fish. They don't have to report shark numbers. That means no one knows how many sharks are caught as bycatch. Andrew Temple is a researcher at Newcastle University in England. He explains, "[There is] a huge discrepancy between the numbers being declared and the actual number being caught—in excess of 2.5 million individual sharks and rays annually."[1]

Each fishing line used in longline fishing has thousands of hooks. Fishers will attach bait to all of the hooks before the line goes in the water.

LONGLINE FISHING

Two commercial fishing methods are extra harmful to sharks. The first is longline fishing. It uses a miles-long fishing line baited with thousands of hooks. Longline fishers are usually trying to catch swordfish or tuna. Those predators eat other fish. That means the bait will also look good to sharks.

The lines for longline fishing are often in the water for a long time. Some species of sharks, such as mako sharks and whale sharks, need to move through water to breathe. If they're trapped on a line, they cannot breathe. When fishers pull in the lines, the sharks are usually dead.

Not all sharks are affected the same way. Tiger sharks can live longer on a longline than many other sharks. So there's a better chance that trapped tiger sharks will be released. But hammerheads, especially endangered scalloped hammerheads, die quickly. Scalloped hammerhead sharks

THE WRONG CATCH

Longlines accidentally catch sharks instead of fish one out of every five times. Since longlines are used around the world, they probably add the most to shark bycatch.

are almost always killed before the longline gets pulled in. Young dusky sharks die 80 percent of the time they're hooked on longlines. Sometimes, fishers find living sharks caught in longlines and free them. But the stress of being caught makes swimming and breathing hard. Even freed sharks can die.

GILLNETS

The second dangerous fishing method is the use of gillnets. These large nets act like a wall in the water. They have small holes that catch on fish's gills. These nets can

A gillnet looks like a net wall in the water. Sea creatures can easily get caught in a gillnet.

kill or hurt many sea creatures, including sharks. Even if a shark gets free, its hurt gills can cause other health problems.

Dusky sharks and great white sharks are often caught in gillnets. Death rates are very high for trapped sharks. Gillnets are extra harmful near coasts, where many species of sharks go to feed and raise their young.

Laws that ban gillnets can help. In 1994, California banned gillnets from coastal waters within 3 miles (4.8 km) of land. Twenty years later, shark species that no one had seen in years had returned to the area. Great white sharks came back. This is

A diver tries to help a dusky shark caught in a net near South Africa.

a good sign for shark populations. A strong shark population shows that the ocean's ecosystem is healthy. Chris Lowe is the director of the Shark Lab at California State University-Long Beach. He says, "You can't have an ecosystem that's badly damaged and have predators."[2]

2

OVERFISHING

It isn't always an accident when people catch sharks. Some fishers are trying to catch them. Many of these sharks will be sold for money. Others are caught for fun. Overfishing is one reason sharks are becoming endangered.

SHARK FISHING

People around the world eat shark meat.

In some countries, it is a **delicacy**.

Sometimes shark meat is sold as what it is.

Freshly caught sharks for sale at an outdoor fish market in Sri Lanka

In other cases, people are eating sharks without knowing it. Shark meat can be hidden in mixed seafood products. In the United Kingdom, some fried fish is made from shark meat. Overfishing of sharks for food has pushed some species closer to extinction.

In the United States, people fish sharks both for fun and for money. Commercial shark fishers use longline fishing and gillnetting. Some shark fishers use strike netting. This method uses gillnets to trap groups of sharks. A plane flies above the ocean. Then the pilot tells fishing boats

Recreational fishers caught this mako shark on purpose. Then they threw it back overboard.

where the sharks are. The boats drop gillnets and capture the sharks. This is a good way to catch sharks quickly. But it is bad for endangered sharks.

A thresher shark caught during a competition called the Monster Shark Fishing Tournament in Cape Cod, Massachusetts

Recreational fishers use normal fishing rods and lines. Shark fishing is legal in the United States. The Atlantic Coast has a long history of fishers competing to catch the biggest sharks. They sometimes release the sharks after taking pictures. This type of fishing is known as catch-and-release. It may not sound bad. But getting pulled out of the water is stressful for a shark. It may not recover after release.

Timing is key to responsible shark fishing. Dr. Vincent Raoult is a marine ecologist. He says that fishers need "to consider the exposure of sharks. Measuring and

Shark fins for sale in a market in Southeast Asia

weighing sharks or posing for social media photos prolongs their exposure and is [harmful] to the animal and potentially fatal in the long run."[3] It's best for the sharks if they are released quickly.

THE SHARK FIN TRADE

Shark finning is even more harmful than fishing contests. This is catching a shark for only one small body part: the dorsal fin. That's the fin on the shark's back. In shark movies, it is often shown poking out of the water.

Shark fins sell for a lot of money. They're used in dishes such as shark fin soup. It's considered a delicacy in some parts of Asia. But this type of fishing is harmful. The fin is a very small portion of the shark. To harvest enough shark fins to make a profit, shark fishers have to catch many sharks.

The process of shark finning isn't pleasant. Fishers catch a shark, cut off its fin, and throw the rest of the shark back in the water. The shark can't swim without its fin, so it sinks to the bottom of the ocean. Then it dies a slow, painful death, either

A longline near Costa Rica accidentally hooked a scalloped hammerhead shark.

from blood loss or from not being able

to breathe.

About 100 million sharks are killed

globally each year. Many are for the shark

fin trade. Shark finning and bycatch have driven scalloped hammerheads to the edge of extinction. In the northwestern Atlantic Ocean, there were over 150,000 scalloped hammerheads in 1981. This population was under 27,000 in 2005. Scientists in other areas have studied scalloped hammerheads since then, but their numbers aren't changing much. The animals are still at risk of dying out.

Since 1994, twenty-two countries have banned shark finning. China is one country where a lot of shark fins are sold. But it has taken steps to reduce shark finning. In

2012, the country banned shark fin soup at government banquets. Andy Cornish directs conservation at the World Wildlife Fund in Hong Kong. He agreed with the change. Cornish said, "This is a very positive step forward. It is the first time that the Chinese central government has expressed a decision to phase out shark fin from banquets funded by taxpayers' money."[4]

FEWER SHARK FIN FOODS

Hong Kong was once the biggest market for shark fins in the world. But by 2019, at least 18,000 hotels had stopped serving shark fin in their restaurants. That and other changes have cut in half the number of shark fins brought into Hong Kong.

3
HABITAT AND HUMANS

Sharks need a healthy environment. But their habitats are threatened by human activities. Pollution and shipping traffic have affected sharks' ocean habitats. And that has pushed some shark species closer to extinction.

POLLUTION

Many shark species live by coasts. They feed and reproduce there. A lot of young sharks use coastal areas as nurseries.

Whale sharks are filter feeders. They suck water into their mouths, and then filters at their throats catch their food. But if trash is in the water, then the whale shark ends up eating that trash, too.

These are safe places to grow up. But humans also live near coasts. So these parts of the ocean are the most polluted. Pollution from cities, farms, and factories all affect the coastal ocean more than the open ocean. That means that shark species that live on the coastline are most affected by pollution.

Pollution harms sharks in a lot of ways. Sharks can become tangled up in ocean trash. They can accidentally eat plastic. Scientists studied a group of bycatch sharks caught near Cornwall, England. They found that 67 percent of this group had eaten plastic. Most of this plastic was fibers from fishing lines and clothing manufacturers.

One way that pollution affects sharks is through bioaccumulation. Sharks are at the top of the food chain. They eat other fish, but not many predators eat them. And the fish that sharks eat have usually eaten smaller fish. The smallest fish

MERCURY

One **toxin** that builds up in sharks is mercury, a heavy metal. Scientists aren't sure why, but mercury doesn't seem to hurt sharks. Yet mercury does affect humans who eat shark meat. In humans, mercury can cause blindness, kidney failure, and loss of hair, nails, and teeth.

might eat mostly plants. The plants likely contain some pollution, or toxins, from the environment. Those toxins stay in the fish's body. When a larger fish eats the small fish, the toxins enter the larger fish's body. The bigger fish will eat many more fish in its lifetime. That means the toxins in its body will continue to increase. Top predators such as sharks eat a lot of large, predatory fish. That means they eat a lot of toxins.

Pollution can also harm coral reefs or other areas where sharks feed. Angel sharks live by the coast. That puts them at high risk from habitat changes. This has led

The endangered angel shark waits on the floor of the ocean. When small fish swim close, the shark pounces and sucks the prey into its mouth.

to some sharks, including the angel shark, becoming critically endangered. That's the highest risk level.

Ships that carry goods through oceans can be dangerous to sharks nearby.

SHIPPING TRAFFIC

When it comes to human-made dangers, coastal sharks get the worst of it. But not all sharks affected by human activities live on coasts. For large creatures, not even the deep ocean is safe. The danger to them comes from shipping traffic.

Most of what people buy is made far from where it is sold. Products are often shipped by sea. Shipping routes are like roads on the open sea. Big cargo ships take the same routes over and over. And just as a car might hit an animal, cargo ships crash into marine life.

Giant creatures such as whales are most affected by cargo ships. But two species of sharks also get hit by ships. The whale shark is the largest fish in the world. It weighs up to 11 tons (10 metric tons) and can be as long as a school bus. The basking shark is the second-largest fish. These can grow up to 40 feet (12 m) long and weigh about 5 tons (4.5 metric tons).

SWIMMING WITH THE SHARKS

Because whale sharks don't hunt, it's safe to swim with them. For many tropical countries, swimming with whale sharks is a major tourism draw. But human contact can be harmful to sharks. Responsible tour groups stay at a safe distance.

Both sharks eat small plants and animals called plankton. Instead of hunting, they swim along the surface of the ocean and filter food through their mouths. That's when they run into ships.

Cargo ships are the largest concern. But near the Maldives, a group of islands in the Indian Ocean, tourist boats often strike whale sharks. Wounds from these accidents can slow a shark's growth. But not all sharks survive, explains whale shark expert Simon Pierce. And no one is counting the sharks that die. Pierce says: "The challenge we've got is assessing

Nurse sharks surround a tourist boat in the Maldives. Sometimes boats in this area hit sharks.

how many sharks are being killed. . . . As whale sharks sink when they die, most mortalities will go unreported."[5] Researchers are still learning how badly ship collisions affect sharks. But they do know that shipping pollution and noise can also harm these animals.

4
PROTECTING SHARKS

Sharks are important to the ocean ecosystem. They eat sick fish, leaving healthier ones. They also keep oceans clean by eating dead fish and plankton. As shark species become endangered, ocean ecosystems can become less healthy. It's not too late to help sharks recover, though.

Many organizations are working to keep sharks from going extinct.

A tiger shark eats a dead sperm whale. The tiger shark is sometimes called the garbage can of the sea, because it will eat whatever it finds.

Harpoon fishing uses a long, sharp tool to spear, or poke, a fish. This produces less bycatch than many other fishing methods.

HOW COUNTRIES CAN PROTECT SHARKS

A good way to protect sharks is to reduce what harms them. Many areas have passed laws to protect sharks from overfishing and bycatch. Two examples are China's shark fin soup ban and California's gillnet ban. In 1991, South Africa passed a law to protect great white sharks. The United Nations banned gillnet fishing on the open seas. In 2000, the United States banned shark finning. And in 2011, the US Congress passed the Shark Conservation Act. This law stated that all sharks caught in US waters must be brought to shore with their fins intact.

Many fisheries are trying to catch the fish they want without catching sharks. They measure water temperature and study the weather to predict where sharks might be. Then they don't fish in those areas.

Some countries are creating shark **sanctuaries**. These are areas where sharks are protected. Shark sanctuaries can help tourism. They also give scientists places to study sharks in their natural habitats. Palau is a nation in the western Pacific Ocean. This country made the first shark sanctuary in 2009. Dermot Keane helped establish it. In 2019, Keane said, "Shark populations at Palau's dive sites have rebounded to healthy and increasing levels."[6]

Palau outlawed shark fishing in its waters in 2009. Snorkelers and scuba divers in the area might see creatures such as gray reef sharks, leopard sharks, or whitetip reef sharks.

HOW PEOPLE CAN HELP SHARKS

One important thing people can do to help sharks is reduce ocean pollution. Single-use plastic, or plastic that gets thrown away after one use, is a big problem. A lot of human trash, including plastic, ends up in the ocean. That can harm sharks and other marine life. Avoiding single-use plastic leads to less plastic in the ocean. If people do use plastic, they should recycle it or throw it away safely.

Shark education is also important. Many people think sharks are dangerous killers, but this is not true. Sharks rarely attack humans, and they are important members of the ecosystem. Educating people can change how they look at sharks.

Some people make art to draw attention to ocean pollution. An artist made this shark sculpture from plastic waste found on beaches.

Humans can also help sharks by buying seafood caught in a **sustainable** way. This means buying from fisheries that are careful

Volunteers gather to clean up a beach in Venezuela. Keeping trash out of the ocean helps the animals that live there.

about bycatch. Not eating shark meat is another way people can help.

Finally, people can help groups that protect the ocean. Anything that helps the ocean also helps sharks and other marine life. Volunteers can help with ocean clean-ups or help share information. Learning about sharks, cleaning up coasts, and reducing plastic use are all acts that can help sharks. If people make the oceans cleaner and safer, endangered sharks can rebuild their numbers. They can become healthier and safer.

CLEANING UP

One group called the Ocean Cleanup built a device to collect tiny bits of plastic in the ocean. As their technology improves, it may clean up a lot of plastic. But most experts agree that keeping plastic out of the ocean in the first place is better for sharks.

GLOSSARY

bycatch
ocean animals that fishers catch accidentally

commercial
having to do with buying and selling things

delicacy
a food item that is special or rare

ecosystem
all the living things in a place and their relationship to one another and their environment

endangered
at risk of dying out, or becoming extinct

recreational
games, sports, and hobbies people do for fun

sanctuaries
nature areas set up to protect animals

sustainable
done in a way that can be continued and doesn't use up natural resources

toxin
a poisonous substance

SOURCE NOTES

CHAPTER ONE: BYCATCH

1. Quoted in Hannah Waters, "Good-Bye Gillnet, Hello Shark Recovery!," *Smithsonian Institution*, September 2014. https://ocean.si.edu.

2. Quoted in Maya L. Kapoor, "White Sharks Rebound in California," *High Country News*, June 24, 2017. www.hcn.org.

CHAPTER TWO: OVERFISHING

3. Quoted in Melissa Cristina Márquez, "Like Shark Fishing? Catch and Release Isn't as Friendly as You Think," *Forbes*, March 2, 2019. www.forbes.com.

4. Quoted in Bettina Wassener, "China Says No More Shark Fin Soup at State Banquets," *New York Times*, July 3, 2012. www.nytimes.com.

CHAPTER THREE: HABITAT AND HUMANS

5. Quoted in Elizabeth Claire Alberts, "Boat Strikes in Maldives Put Pressure on Whale Sharks' Survival Odds," *Mongabay*, January 29, 2021. https://news.mongabay.com.

CHAPTER FOUR: PROTECTING SHARKS

6. Quoted in Jen Sawada, "How Shark Sanctuaries Sparked a Conservation Movement," *Pew Charitable Trusts*, April 1, 2019. www.pewtrusts.org.

FOR FURTHER RESEARCH

BOOKS

William McKeever, *Emperors of the Deep: Sharks—The Ocean's Most Mysterious, Most Misunderstood, and Most Important Guardians*. San Francisco, CA: HarperOne, 2020.

Oceanology: The Secrets of the Seas Revealed. London: DK, 2020.

Brian Skerry, *The Ultimate Book of Sharks*. Washington, DC: National Geographic, 2018.

INTERNET SOURCES

Helen Briggs, "Extinction: 'Time Is Running Out' to Save Sharks and Rays," *BBC*, January 27, 2021. www.bbc.com.

Katie Hogge, "9 Ways to Help Sharks This Shark Week," *Ocean Conservancy*, July 31, 2019. www.oceanconservancy.org.

Ben Panko, "More Than a Third of Shark Species Are Now Threatened with Extinction," *Smithsonian Magazine*, September 8, 2021. www.smithsonianmag.com.

WEBSITES

The International Union for the Conservation of Nature (IUCN)
www.iucn.org

The IUCN is dedicated to preserving nature and endangered species. It maintains the IUCN Red List, which categorizes species based on how close they are to extinction.

The Ocean Conservancy
www.oceanconservancy.org

The Ocean Conservancy is focused on protecting the ocean and marine species against human-caused threats such as climate change and pollution. Its website includes articles about ocean conservation.

World Wildlife Fund
www.worldwildlife.org

The World Wildlife Fund is dedicated to preserving wildlife. It hosts news articles and informational articles about endangered species, including sharks, on its website.

INDEX

angel sharks, 40–41

basking sharks, 44–45
bioaccumulation, 39–40

catch-and-release fishing, 29–31
China, 34–35, 51
coasts, 21, 29, 37–38, 40, 43, 57
commercial fishing, 12, 17, 24, 26, 32
Cornish, Andy, 35

dusky sharks, 19, 21

eating shark meat, 25–26, 32, 35, 39, 56
ecosystem, 11, 23, 48, 54

filter feeders, 37, 45

gillnets, 19–21, 26–27, 51
great white sharks, 6–8, 21, 51

Hong Kong, 35

Keane, Dermot, 52

laws, 21, 34–35, 50–51, 53
longline fishing, 16–19, 26, 33
Lowe, Chris, 23

mako sharks, 17, 27
Maldives, 45–47
mercury, 39

ocean cleanups, 56–57

Palau, 52, 53
Pierce, Simon, 45–47
plastic, 38–39, 53–54, 55, 57
pollution, 11, 36, 37–40, 47, 53–54

Raoult, Vincent, 29–31
recreational fishing, 11, 24, 26, 27, 29

sanctuaries, 52
scalloped hammerhead sharks, 18–19, 33, 34
Shark Conservation Act, 51
shark finning, 30, 31–35, 51
shipping traffic, 36, 42, 43–47
South Africa, 22, 51
strike netting, 26–27

Temple, Andrew, 15
tiger sharks, 18, 49
tourism, 44, 45, 46, 52

whale sharks, 17–18, 37, 44–47

IMAGE CREDITS

Cover: © Wildest Animal/Shutterstock Images
5: © Nickalbi/iStockphoto
7: © Stefan Pircher/Shutterstock Images
9: © Sebastian Castelier/Shutterstock Images
10: © Red Line Editorial
13: © Andreas Altenburger/Shutterstock Images
14: © Sergey and Marina Pyataev/Shutterstock Images
16: © Thomas Pajot/Shutterstock Images
20: © Damsea/Shutterstock Images
22: © Jeff Rotman/Alamy
25: © Andreas Wolochow/Shutterstock Images
27: © Fiona Ayerst/Shutterstock Images
28: © Michael Matthews/Alamy
30: © Maximillian Cabinet/Shutterstock Images
33: © Jeff Rotman/Blue Planet Archive
37: © Rich Carey/Shutterstock Images
41: © Martin Voeller/iStockphoto
42: © Alexey Seafarer/Shutterstock Images
46: © Sun Shine/Shutterstock Images
49: © James D. Watt/Blue Planet Archive
50: © Jue Worn/Shutterstock Images
53: © Ethan Daniels/Shutterstock Images
55: © Hannah Rudd/Shutterstock Images
56: © Edgloris Marys/Shutterstock Images

ABOUT THE AUTHOR

Elisa A. Bonnin was born and raised in the Philippines. She later moved to the United States to study chemistry and then oceanography. After completing her doctorate, she moved to Germany to work as a scientist. She also writes young adult fiction and nonfiction.